MY LETTERS TO PRESIDENT OBAMA:
Confessions of a Compulsive Letter Writer

By

Jim Green

DEDICATED TO:

April and Tod, My grandchildren--Dylan and Chloe,
And all who want to make the world a better place

ISBN-10: 1477578129

MY LETTERS TO PRESIDENT OBAMA: Confessions of a Compulsive Letter Writer

PROLOGUE

Best guess is that I have written in excess of 500 letters, and counting, to President Obama since he was sworn in on January 20, 2009—on some occasions I have written two letters in one day—this is a sampling of those letters.

Compulsive letter writers, incidentally, do not go looking for a computer/word-processor—they look up and one magically appears before them—and more often than not they have no idea how they got there [only a slight exaggeration]—

While my letters to President Obama contain suggestions as well as constructive criticism—it needs to be said at the beginning that never in a million years would I vote to put a Republican back in the White House!

The agenda of the national Republican Party has not changed one iota since 1980—and has, singularly, brought on all of the symptoms characteristic during the Fall of The Roman Empire—i.e., their corrupt and unworkable policies have almost destroyed America!

The best explanation I can find for why anyone would vote for a Republican for president [apparently Romney] was offered by Gore Vidal who observed that we are the "United States of Amnesia"—

We have a segment of Americans who are racists and would never vote for President Obama because he is black—but another component in this "anti-Obama" faction are persons with a severe memory loss [all else being equal] and have forgotten the destruction done to America—by Bush's appointment to the presidency!

If America does fail it will have two parents: GREED and IGNORANCE—Greed on the part of the 1%, and Ignorance on the part of those in the 99%--who are ignorant of the Republican agenda to replace our Democracy, with a Plutocracy—[i.e., to relegate American to the 8th Century]-

And with the five unscrupulous Republican ideologues on our Supreme Court--who sold our democracy, and America, down the river by handing a blank check to the 1% in "Citizens United"—The 1% can now, theoretically, buy our elections and put a dictator, or a common thief, in the White House—

This Decision has gutted our current election laws in America, and the outcome of this horrid Decision is a glaring unknown—its mere existence may well signal that American is finished!

Regarding constructive criticism of the Obama Administration—the criticism has focused on essential changes in two major areas [one barely on the Radar, the other in the headlines daily]:

Specifically, the establishment of "Fail-Safe" electronic voting in every jurisdiction in America; and Jobs.

Admittedly, the Administration was forced to spend every waking moment focused on rescuing America from the corrupt and disastrous Republican policies which almost drove our economy into another Great Depression--

But we had a very narrow window when the Democrats controlled the Senate, House and White House and had the opportunity to fix the above—but blew it--and the failure to do so cost the Democrats the 2010 election— and may well cost President Obama re-election to the White House in 2012—

The letters to follow will articulate both the problem, and the proposed solution—[one is a Letter to the editor]—the objective is to communicate re topical issues....

But to touch briefly on the need for "fail-safe" electronic voting machines [hereafter EVM]—what we currently have is a nightmare—With the EVM manufacturers claiming proprietary ownership of the software to count our votes—with known computer manipulation such as "vote-flipping" and "under-votes", and with one manufacturer making a $200, 000 contribution to Bush in 2004, and "guaranteeing" Bush Ohio in 2004! And to top it off--no paper trail for a legitimate recount, or to verify how we voted!

To use a metaphor:

Visualize that Wal-Mart handed us a piece of paper with the words "trust us" as a receipt for our purchases—and you will have a consummate understanding of our current electronic voting, in America—In short, did

Kerry really lose in 2004—are you really sure? And did the Republicans really give the Democrats a "shellacking" in 2010?

If Wal-Mart did this, incidentally, we would be outraged—but unfortunately far too many Americans are ignorant [or too trusting] of the dangers indigenous to this EVM nightmare—and yet, there is far more at stake than a complaint with Wal-Mart--it is our democracy that is on the chopping block in this case!

Incidentally, the caption on my letters to President Obama almost always read: President Obama/Fellow Democrats, and concluded with Jim Green, Democrat candidate for Congress, 2000—which I hoped would give it at least a little more chance of being read—by anyone—[also, the quoted unemployment rate was current at the time—letters are not in sequence].

Also, initially, I addressed to F. Michael Kelleher—Special assistant to President Obama who sorted out letters for

President Obama to read—but letters, there, are limited to 2500 words—and I couldn't get all I wanted to say in, and also include the address to Mr. Kelleher—so had to abbreviate my salutation, as above. [Reader: Please look for the nuggets, if you sense redundancy]….Finally, I have no idea if any of my letters were ever read by President Obama.

CHAPTER ONE: Jobs

President Obama/Fellow Democrats:

For the past 65 years we have had two parallel paths to address unemployment in America—

To assure employment for the troops returning from WW II, President Truman signed into law The Full Employment Act of 1946—

This was expanded upon in 1978 with the Humphrey-Hawkins Full Employment Act, signed into law by President Carter—

And a 21st Century version of this path to full employment in America, is pending the House, HR 870.

Humphrey-Hawkins best defines this path to addressing unemployment in America, and it "authorizes" our government to create a "reservoir of public employees" anytime our unemployment rises above "3%".

And in spite of the fact that this path to employment has been the law of the land since 1946—and is a Pro-Market solution [more on this shortly]---Washington has lacked the wherewithal to implement this path to employment on behalf of the American people—[a point not lost on the "occupy" movement].

Rather, Washington has taken the alternate parallel path—by insisting that human labor is a "component" in the free enterprise system—[barely distinguishable from the machine the human operates] to be used and discarded "at will"—and the Republican propaganda is that it is an attack upon "freedom" to challenge this concept, but whose "freedom"?

As a result, however, "conventional wisdom" has insisted that it is the market, alone, that can fix our unemployment crisis—the result has been a disaster—

The market thrives when we have a robust, employed, consuming public—and by taking this parallel path—we not only have a staggering 8.1% unemployment, but a struggling recovery as well.

Ironically, following WW II, Australia passed a law very similar to our Full Employment Act of 1946—

Difference is—they actually put it into effect—and over the next 30 years—[until the cold winds of conservatism swept in Reagan and Thatcher, etc.] –the government in Australia saw as a solemn responsibility that "anyone willing to work should be provided with a job" [a quote from the "Audacity of Hope"].

The citizens of Australia still refer to this 30 years as their "Golden Age".

Jim Green, Democrat candidate for Congress, 2000
www.Inclusivism.org

Editor, NY TIMES

The only way any person could "disapprove" of the way President Obama is handling the job—are persons who have not informed themselves with the facts—or are suffering from severe amnesia—or both—

Republican policies had handed President Obama an economy in shambles when he took office in 2009—and we had lost 2.6 million jobs in 2008, alone, the highest job loss in six decades!

We can't siphon America's wealth out of the hands of the consuming middle, the 99%--and transfer it into the hands of the Republican's wealthiest contributors, the 1% [via obscene tax cuts]—without sending our economy into meltdown.

This is based on common sense—The consuming middle stops buying the products made by our manufacturers,

when they don't have enough money—and in the
domino effect our manufacturers lay off their employees
when they don't have consumers for their products—
and on and on until our economy is in shamble.

And those who inform themselves know that
Reaganomics [what Bush I called "VooDoo economics"]
has a shelf-life of about seven years before the economy
collapses—as it did in 1987, and again in 2008—

And the taxpayers have to rush in with tons of cash, as
Bush did with TARP in 2008, and an equal amount by
President Obama--to prevent another Great Depression.

Also, with each new cycle of this economic scheme—the
bail out has grown larger and larger—

For instance, in 1987—when the stock market lost one-
fourth of its value on Black Monday, October 19,
1987—the bailout was in the hundreds of bilions—in
2008, the bailout has been in the trillions of dollars, and

counting--to mop up the mess caused by this failed economic agenda!

In short, President Obama did not spend the tons of cash [and as Bush did with TARP]—because he is a wild "tax and spend" liberal—and as our racists and Republican ideologues would have our uninformed believe—

Both Obama and Bush went to the only doctor in town for a prescription [cash and plenty of it] to rescue America from another Great Depression!

Further, when any of the Republicans in Washington rail against our deficit, who voted to cause it—as Paul Ryan did under Bush II—is a hypocrite!

Romney has made it clear, in no uncertain terms, that he intends to pickup where Bush II left off—i.e., to pander to the GREED of the Republican's richest contributors at the expense of the 99% rest of us—it is the Republican One and Only program—

Jim Green, Democrat candidate for Congress, 2000 [see THE HARVARD BOYS CLUB, on Amazon]

President Obama/Fellow Democrats:

Who thought up the idea that the "Market" could solve our unemployment crisis?

The greatest enemy to our economic recovery is the archaic mind-set that it is ONLY the "Market" that can create jobs—

It has been a stumbling block to job creation—

It has been a stumbling block to market recovery—

It may also be a stumbling block to President Obama's re-election—

Going forward—the market will not provide enough jobs, which bears repeating—

Going forward—the market will not provide enough jobs—

Which raises the question: Does the government [under law "We The People"] have a responsibility to step up on behalf of the American people when the market does not provide enough jobs?

And according to the vast majority of "We The People" – "anybody willing to work should be able to find a job" [and the message loud and clear by the "occupy" movement]—

In short, the answer to that question is a resounding: YES

What apparently isn't clear going forward is that an expanding and contracting public workforce is an INDISPENSABLE component to a modern market economy—

This is a Pro-Market "win-win" solution—the American people win, and capitalism wins—

Jim Green, Democrat candidate for Congress, 2000
www.Inclusivism.org YouTube: JGREEN56789

President Obama/Fellow Democrats:

I am a fan. I am 110% in favor of Democrats succeeding—and in a post mortem:

Had we fixed unemployment, everything we did over the past two years would have been seen only in a most positive light [and the Tea Party would have been holding their rallies in a phone booth]—but when we failed to fix—we were seen as not being able to do anything right!

To fix our unemployment crisis in America, we must totally remove the problem from our market economy model—and look upon it, as we rightfully should—as a "social" problem, in search of a social solution—

That is, in looking for a solution, no differently than our methodology for seeking better ways to educate our youth, or fight disease—a social problem in search of a solution—and the sooner we alter direction, the better—

For instance, our current solutions [HR 2847, etc., -- warmed over Reaganomics]—look upon humans as a "commodity", rather than an "asset" –and the result of going down this path has been a disaster, and has resulted in our unemployment crisis getting even worse!

This erroneous path also cost the Democrats the House, and resulted in a greatly weakened Senate, in the mid-terms!

A very clear mandate from the public in 2008 was FIX UNEMPLOYMENT—and when the Democrats failed to do this [mostly as a result of bad advice]—the public turned their back on the Democrats, and saw us as weak or incompetent, or both!

And all the while we had the solution at our fingertips in a win/win solution [both the public and capitalism wins]—in the pro-market Humphrey–Hawkins Full Employment Act which authorizes the government/president to create a "reservoir of public employment" anytime our unemployment in America exceeds "3%"—

And we are three times over the percent necessary to trigger this Federal Law—[at 9.8% unemployment]—but can fix overnight without adding a dime to our deficit—www.Inclusivism.org—had we taken the right path]!

And all of our errors could have been avoided from day one had we looked upon unemployment as a "social" problem—in search of a social solution---in short, we Democrats had our chance—and we muffed it—

Jim Green, Democrat candidate for Congress, 2000

President Obama/Fellow Democrats:

In his new book "The Grand Design", Stephen Hawking observed," To understand the universe at its deepest level, we need to know not only how the universe behaves, but why."

And the same is true to answer why did we take the wrong path to address our unemployment crisis in America—[and paid dearly at the polls --it is impossible to have 9-17% unemployment and even remotely suggest that we are on the right path]!

And the question posed here is: Why did our "brightest and best"—AKA "conventional wisdom" unwittingly take the Obama administration down the wrong path [HR 2847—failed Reaganomics]—all [except Republicans] wanted Obama to succeed in fixing unemployment—

This is one man's opinion re the why our "brightest and best" got it so wrong:

First and foremost, they have a mental blinder to seeing any avenue to fix unemployment—except "via the market"—[i.e., classical economics—based on the "dollar' rather than on "humans"]—and even though the path we should be on is virtually right under their nose-- because of blinders—it is impossible for them to see it--

That is, they are looking for a solution through a false prism—the false prism is that jobs can only be created, as noted, via the "market"—when, in fact, the "market" is the worst place for us to look to solve our unemployment crisis—

For instance, fixing unemployment is antithetical to the objectives of capitalism—unemployment is a "social" problem—and the objectives of capitalism is to make a "profit" –the market only hires persons as a means to increase profits—not to address social problems--

Indeed, every waking moment in capitalism is spent pondering ways to eliminate as many of us humans, as possible, from the workplace—to increase "profits"--

Another illustration of our "brightest and best" being blind-sided—Dr. Robert B. Reich is a progressive—and yet in his book "The Work of Nations"—he does not make even one reference to the Humphrey-Hawkins Full Employment Act—which authorizes the government to create a "reservoir of public employment" anytime our unemployment exceeds "3%"— see also: www.Inclusivism.org

That is, he failed to understand that this IS the answer—this is the path we should be on to fix an unemployment crisis because it is an indispensable component to a modern market economy…it is a pro-market solution--that is, it is a "win-win" solution--the people win, and capitalism wins….

Jim Green, Democrat candidate for Congress, 2000

Reagan was a horrible prez—so why the LIES?

President Obama/Fellow Democrats:

What are we to make of a president who wanted to do the right thing—and probably thought [most of the time] he was doing the right thing—but, in fact, was a horrible president—and, in fact, did substantial harm to America—

The mystery president--and evident by the HBO movie by the same name "Reagan"—who was, without question, the worst president in American history--until Bush II came along and bumped him out of last place—

Problem is—Conservatives/Republicans are currently trying to re-write history—to give us—THE AMERICAN PEOPLE—a pure BS image of Reagan—one where he is elevated to sainthood—it is the "Big Lie"—

Indeed, on this very day [3-2-2011] House Majority Leader Eric Cantor was still trying to pull the wool over the eyes of the American people with the same BS line used re Reaganomics:

Eliminate all of the social progress since FDR, and cut, even further, taxes on the top 2% [the only people Cantor—or any of the other Republicans in Congress Represent—they certainly do not represent the best interests of the 98% rest of us Americans]—

But if we do this jobs will flow like wine—

What a CROCK---in short, Cantor wants to slam on the brakes during a sluggish recovery—which, with a virtual certainty, will destroy our recovery and destroy jobs in America! Reaganomics has a shelf-life of about 7 years before the evaporation of wealth from the consuming middle, and its false premise starts caving in on itself: Proof-1987/2008

So when are the Democrats going to stand up and have the guts to say—NO MORE—no more "me too"--no more Reagan lies—no more harming America—and stand up on behalf of the American people?

We can end our unemployment crisis in the next 6 months—[See: www.Inclusivism.org] --but we have to stand up—we have to show some backbone—show some spine—When are we Democrats going to stand up and tell the American people the truth—that Reaganomics is DooDoo BRAINS!

Jim Green, Democrat candidate for Congress, 2000

WHERE IS OUR "UN-AMERICAN" INVESTIGATION INTO THE REPUBLICAN AGENDA? WHERE IS THE REPUBLICAN APOLOGY?

President Obama/Fellow Democrats:

We need to restore the "Un–American Activities Committee" and put the Republicans in the Senate and House, et al –– on trial for selling out the American people, and America––by pandering to the GREED of their richest contributors—their One and Only program!

For instance, the Republican "job creation" solution, today, is the same old cruel joke they have been perpetrating on the American people since the first Bush tax cuts in 2001—

The joke goes like this: Pour obscene tons of cash [the taxpayers money] on our richest contributors—and they will use the money to give everyone a job—supposedly in the corporation—

Well, if this worked—why do we have 14 million Americans still unemployed? [The Bush tax cuts were extended]!

What really happened is that their richest contributors used the obscene windfall of cash to buy a bigger yacht, or take extra trips to Europe—rather than create jobs—as their wealth doubled at the expense of the 98% of the rest of us Americans!

And it makes you wonder how the Republicans in the Senate and House can espouse this joke with a straight face! Fool me once-----

Further, we learned from this that siphoning America's wealth from our consuming middle has a shelf-life of about 7 years before our economy goes into a nosedive—[1987 & 2008]—and in 2008 brought us dangerously close to another Great Depression!

And compounded by the fact that the Republicans ran up massive deficits on Americans, when they have held the White House since 1980—to make up for the shortfall in revenue-—creating a dual crisis: Massive debt as well as high unemployment—and has put America in extreme economic peril!

In short, the current Republican agenda poses far more of threat to Americans, and America—than terrorists!

If this isn't the quintessential definition of "un-American", what is? And the only question left is do we have a Democrat in Washington with the guts to step up to the plate and initiate this committee—i.e., pull back the curtain so that the American people can see the Republican's real agenda?

Jim Green, Democrat candidate for Congress, 2000
www.Inclusivism.org

President Obama/Fellow Democrats--

There is a famous line from F. Scott Fitzgerald's "The Great Gatsby" regarding the carelessness of Tom and Daisy---a wealthy couple—and I'll paraphrase--they "smash up things and then retreat back into their money, leaving it to others to clean up their mess"

Is this not the quintessential definition of the Republican Party over the past 30 years?

U.S. Representative Ron Paul, a doctrinaire Libertarian— in an interview on CNN 4-21-11-- was more pointed when he asserted that we played right into bin Laden's hand—squandering our wealth in America on Iraq and Afghanistan, etc.—and bringing our economy to the brink of collapse—finished bin Laden's attack on 9-11-

And whether bin Laden could actually read us that well--—Congressman Paul was dead-on correct with the end result—

Further, our economic collapse in 1987 should have served as fair warning that Supply–Side Economics has a shelf–life of only about 7 years before the economy starts caving in on itself—

We can't siphon America's wealth away from the consuming middle—the 98% of us [by giving obscene tax cuts for the top 2%] without sending our economy into a tailspin!

But by not learning from this lesson, we had to relive it again in 2008—only this time it created the worst economic disaster since the Great Depression!

And in the greatest shift upward of wealth in our history at present—400 persons now hold more of American's wealth than 150 million of the rest of us do!

Further, we need to remind the Republicans in the Senate and House who espouse, daily, that cutting taxes for the

2% will solve our unemployment crisis [the Republican's One and Only job creation solution]—That this is what we are doing NOW—[the tax cuts were extended] and it has left us with 14 million Americans still unemployed!

And finally, how anyone could buy into Congressman Paul Ryan's deficit reduction plan—Supply-Side Economics on steroids—is beyond human comprehension!

Jim Green, Democrat candidate for Congress, 2000
www.Inclusivism.org

F. Michael Kelleher, Special Assistant to the President

President Obama/Fellow Democrats:

Only 20% of Americans have the "deficit" as their highest priority for Congress to fix—while according to a recent Zogby poll "86% of Americans think the government should provide a job to anyone who wants one".

In short, Job Creation is overwhelmingly more important to the American people, at present, than the deficit—and yet, *all* of the political focus in Washington has shifted from our unemployment crisis [with almost 14 million Americans still unemployed] --to the "deficit"—

Which should cause all of us to question, and perhaps with more than a little alarm: When did this happen, and why did this happen?

And the "When" appears to have two parents: when the 2010 election brought in a wrath of radical Republicans

[AKA Tea Party] –with an anti-government "starve the beast" mind–set—and when President Obama appointed a "deficit commission" rather than a "job creation commission"—[perhaps, believing HR 2847 was a solution—when, in fact, it has been a miserable failure!].

It was a decision Democrats would live to regret—given the mandate by the American people in 2008: Fix Unemployment! Had we fixed unemployment--every bill passed by we Democrats, including healthcare reform, would have been bullet-proof—but when we didn't, everything we did became a target.

With the end result that we got hammered in the 2010 election—and a "radical" plan [Ryan] which would destroy Medicare Insurance—and the "Big Lie" according to Eliot Spitzer, by the Republicans in Congress, that "cutting marginal [tax] rates for those at the top will create jobs" [when THIS IS WHAT WE ARE DOING NOW—the tax cuts were extended!]--

To put in perspective: We have 20 years, and hard work, to fix the deficit—but we have 5 minutes to fix our unemployment crisis—As Harry Hopkins noted in the 30's "People don't eat some day, they eat every day"!

So how do we Democrats wrest America back from this dangerous sabotage—and re-set the agenda to what Americans want us to focus on: Job Creation?

A good start would be for the administration to get behind Rep Conyers' 21st Century Humphrey Hawkins Bill, currently in committee in the House.

Jim Green, Democrat candidate for Congress, 2000
www.Inclusivism.org

President Obama/Fellow Democrats:

When on earth did our policy makers get locked into the notion that our "only" source of jobs in America is from the "private sector"? Or that this is even the best source of jobs—it is a sacred cow that, at present, has locked 14 million Americans out of a job!

When every waking moment in capitalism is spent pondering ways to eliminate as many of us humans, as possible, from the workforce—to increase "profits"— Why on earth would we look to this model to solve our unemployment crisis in America?

It would be ideal if the market would absorb everyone in—but it never has, and it never will!

Further, this "sacred cow" injures capitalism, as well as the unemployed! The market thrives when we have a robust, employed, consuming workforce!

We have a lot of definitions of what "The American Dream" means—mine is, "Make a better paperclip, sell it for a million bucks, and retire in south Florida"— so notions that this is an anti-capitalism tyrant is sheer poppycock!

It is our "sacred cow"—that jobs can only come from the private sector--that is anti-capitalism!

And this sacred cow is also the reason why our policy makers embrace the bizarre notion—and have committed hundreds of billions of the taxpayers money to this folly----that "small business" will fix our unemployment crisis!

It would be impossible to have 14 million Americans [almost 1 in 10 of our workforce] still unemployed—if these laws actually worked!

It is clearly plausible that public and private sector jobs can work in concert—indeed, embracing pubic sector employment will create more private sector jobs in 6 months, than HR 2847 [The HIRE ACT] in 6 years—so what is our aversion to public sector jobs?

This is not suggesting that public sector jobs would be employed by the federal government, but rather that a fund would be created to fund the millions of jobs, in every jurisdiction in America that every year go unfilled, for lack of funding—See: www.Inclusivism.org

The fact is, we have far more jobs that need to be done in America—than persons to fill these jobs—so public sector jobs are a "win-win"—the American people win, and capitalism wins!

It is currently projected by the IMF that China is going to pass up the American economy in 2016—while we cling to our "sacred cow" to the last burning ember--

The world has changed, our solutions haven't, and the result for America--is disastrous--

Jim Green, Democrat candidate for Congress, 2000

President Obama/Fellow Democrats:

I cannot help but think that the biting criticism of President Obama—by Princeton Professor Cornel West—relates to the golden opportunity the Obama administration/Democrats had to end pervasive unemployment in America—and particularly as this adversely impacts minorities—and the Obama administration let this golden opportunity slip by and is now stuck with a window that may well be closed.

At the beginning of the Obama administration the American public extended an open hand and was expecting and welcomed "bold experimentation"—we wanted results and were convinced the Obama administration could produce results. And if we recall, Americans were saying "Fix Unemployment" long before the Bush meltdown infinitely compounded the problem.

But the administration got bad advice—and locked into a mind-set that "private sector jobs" could end our unemployment crisis—it would be ideal if the market would provide everyone with a job—but the empirical evidence is indisputable—"private sector jobs" can never more than make a dent in our unemployment—and a tiny dent at that—and if the data from Fareed Zakaria is correct we still have 25 million Americans without work—two years down our current path—in sum, the world has changed, our solutions haven't, and result has been disastrous--

It is impossible to say we are on the right path if we have 25 million Americans still unemployed, and sadly the open hand at the beginning became a closed fist in the 2010 election—when our unemployment had barely ticked downward—and at $2.5 million for every private sector job created--our current path became a cost-effective nightmare.

The public interchanges the words "economy" and "unemployment" and even in our modest recovery the public perception is that our economy is doing poorly, and rates the Obama administration accordingly on the economy—because we did not fix unemployment.

In the alternative, if at the beginning--the administration would have acted on the authority under Humphrey-Hawkins to create a "reservoir of public employment" –with the target provided in this law to reduce unemployment to "3%"—all of the good works by the Obama administration since –would have been bullet-proof, rather than—as it has turned out—including the disappointment of Professor West—a target—

There is a maxim "It is never too late to do the right thing" and Representative Conyers has introduced a latter-day Humphrey-Hawkins Bill – HR 870 [currently in Committee in the House]—and we fund without adding a dime to our deficit. See also: www.Inclusivism.org

Jim Green, Democrat candidate for Congress, 2000

President Obama/Fellow Democrats:

Ending our unemployment crisis in America is comparable to getting bin Laden, to the 10th power--

The Obama administration has a real shot at ending our unemployment crisis in America by getting behind HR 870, introduced by Congressman Conyers [currently in Committee]—

And "0" chance by staying on our current path—with HR 2847 costing the taxpayers $2.5 million per each $9 per hour "private sector job" created—and virtually no change in our unemployment rate--

A large part of the problem is that we have been duped by right-wing propaganda—that has sabotaged an effective solution, and the American people—more on this shortly--

Gore Vidal asserts America is amnesic re our history--
and we need to recall that unemployment was the
number one political issue in America—Before the Bush
economic meltdown took the problem into a whole new
orbit—

The truth is, the problem is systemic, and calls for a
systemic solution—the world has changed, our solutions
haven't, and as a result--the path we are currently
following has been disastrous!

We need to mark the source of our current
unemployment crisis back to around 1975, give or
take—when the colliding forces of globalization,
automation, etc., reached a critical mass—resulting in
ubiquitous unemployment—in short, we became victims
of our progress--

Our response to the malaise in the 70's, caused by
pervasive unemployment in America, was the

Humphrey-Hawkins Full Employment Act, in 1978 [hereafter H–H].

Specifically, this law authorizes the government to create a "reservoir of public employees"—any time our unemployment rises above "3%" – i.e., it is a Pro-Market solution that can be funded without adding a dime to our deficit: i.e., two examples, HR 870/ www.Inclusivism.org

To undermine H–H, in 1979, a wealthy ultra-right foundation funded a fraudulent study by a student at MIT [with no background in economics]—which asserted that "small business private sector jobs" would provide all the jobs needed in America—[to sabotage a government role in fixing our pervasive unemployment] and the foundation then spent millions of dollars promoting this fraudulent concept!

Our proof that this concept doesn't work: It would be impossible to have 14–25 million Americans still unemployed if this flawed study was correct—because we bought into it hook, line and sinker—it is the premise we are foolishly following at present to fix our unemployment crisis--

Jim Green, Democrat candidate for Congress, 2000

RE: Press conference 7/11/11

President Obama/Fellow Democrats:

WHY ON GOD'S EARTH WOULD SOCIAL SECURITY INSURANCE BE A PART OF THE DEFICITS CAUSED BY IRRESPONSIBLE AND RECKLESS REPUBLICAN POLICIES OF THE PAST 30 YEARS?

Why on earth would we put a self-sustaining Insurance program—[Social Security] that brings in more money than it pays out—be "on the table"?

It has nothing to do with the "deficit"—and those who complain about paying interest on the moneys stolen from the Social Security Trust Fund—or somehow link this to our current deficit problem—should be incarcerated for Fraud and Theft!

There is an argument for long-term restructuring so that Social Security Insurance is sustainable after 2037—an actuarial restructuring common to all insurance—but to say that we just must do this before August 2, 2011 is patently insane!

Medicare is also an INSURANCE program. As a senior I pay almost $100 a month for Medicare—I am 77 and so far the government is ahead of the game—but the problem with Medicare Insurance is much different than our actuarial problem in 2037.

Medicare Insurance has both long and short-term problems because of waste, fraud and "for profit" profiteers robbing it blind! I am a capitalist—I totally support build a better widget, sell it for a million bucks, and retire in South Florida—but making a "profit" from the healthcare of another human should be a criminal offense!

Finally, why is the word "entitlement" being thrown around like a drunken sailor when referring to the Social Security and Medicare INSURANCE programs?

"Entitlement" was invented by wing-nuts in the 1970's—to be derisive—to suggest that these INSURANCE programs are giveaway programs of some kind—do we refer to our auto insurance as an "entitlement"?

Every time anyone in our government or media refers to Social Security and Medicare INSURANCE as an "entitlement" they are deferring to our wing-nuts—to our lowest common denominator—our scumbags, to be frank—persons who are NOT committed to building a safe and sane America in which to live and raise our children—

President Obama: Our constitution mandates that Congress MUST pay our "Debts"—it is not an either/or--The Republicans caused this debt and are now trying to renege on payment and to hold the American people hostage so they can undermine Social Security and Medicare—and you can end this circus via Executive Order—on behalf of the American people--

Jim Green, Democrat candidate for Congress, 2000

www.Inclusivism.org

ATTN: Austan Goolsby – The White House

With all due respect to the road metaphor--rather than an innocuous "bump in the road" sign, it should read "bridge out ahead" as a warning to us Democrats that we are on the wrong road to solve our unemployment crisis in America—

When we have 14-25 million Americans still unemployed [depending on economist] it is impossible to disregard that the world has changed, our solutions haven't, and the result has been disastrous--

—It is the "opinion" of "conventional wisdom" that the best way to fix our unemployment crisis—is with "private sector jobs"— and cling to this notion like a ticket on the Titanic -- insisting we are on the right road—

And as a result we have crafted our legislation– and committed billions of the taxpayers dollars around this erroneous concept --to make this opinion come true—

But the bottom line is: What We Are Doing Isn't Working!

Another component of this—the public sees as synonymous and inter-changeable terms "economy" and "employment"— and which the Republicans are more than happy to exploit—

For instance, when Romney declares President Obama has done a miserable job with the economy [even though it was a masterful job on one level]—the public agrees with Romney—because we have not fixed our unemployment crisis—and in spite of the fact that Bush's economic meltdown made the problem infinitely worse—

Our unemployment dilemma dates to the mid-70's, and the Humphrey-Hawkins Full Employment Act [15 USC § 3101] signed into law by President Carter, correctly assesses the solution essential in a modern economy—a solution that is both pro-market, and addresses the social crisis caused by unemployment.

Specifically, the government/president is "authorized" to create a "reservoir of public employment"—at any time out unemployment rate exceeds "3%"—[and we are three times over the percent necessary to trigger this law]—Additionally, Rep. Conyers has picked up the banner with HR 870 [currently in Committee]—and it is inexplicable why it is being disregarded—

Further, there are various deficit-neutral methods to fund a public workforce, please see: HR 870 – www.Inclusivism.org

Will the Republicans try to undermine – is the Pope a Catholic – but the public wants to chip in and supports a

Neighbor-To-Neighbor Job Creation Act—and the
Republicans need to exposed for opposing job creation—

This is a "win-win" solution—the American people win,
and capitalism wins—

Jim Green, Democrat candidate for Congress, 2000

President Obama/Fellow Democrats:

On June 13, 2011—Larry Summers, President Obama's first, and former, Director of the National Economic Council, projected that our unemployment rate should be down to 8% before the 2012 election—

Based on this projection we can definitively say that as an advisor on "unemployment"—[and in particular during the Great Recession]—President Obama could have gotten worse advice from his top economic advisor—but it is difficult to see how—

Professor Summers was brilliant in understanding the fix re our investment banking, but horrible in his understanding the cause and results of unemployment-- And we have 24 million Americans unemployed or underemployed as proof!

There is no rational explanation why our unemployment rate in America, today, should exceed 3%—None—

Had Director Summers [our "conventional wisdom"] actually understood this social/economic/political problem and how to solve it—

We would have had legislation in the hopper and/or enforced existing legislation [15 USC § 3101]-- within the first 90 days, and we Americans would have been well on our way to 3% unemployment by the end of 2009—

Further, had this been the case, the American people, currently, would be considering an amendment to our Constitution so that President Obama could serve more than two terms—rather than seriously considering limiting to one—

To illustrate, we would never condemn the CEO for closing a plant, if they are losing money—but the American people are outraged by a government that lacks the imagination and wherewithal to step up to the plate with a solution to this lapse in our market system—

And at present we are asking the market to fix itself with both hands tied behind its back—by inexplicably, looking upon government involvement as if it were the plague, and insisting upon solving our unemployment crisis with "private sector jobs"—a concept that is antithetical to capitalism!

Full Employment is a Pro-Market concept—the market thrives when we have a robust, employed, consuming public – and we have far more jobs that need to be done in America, in every jurisdiction in America, than we have persons to fill these jobs—

While America drowns in myths and sacred cows-

The bottom line is, HR 870 [currently in Committee] can fix our unemployment crisis without adding a dime to our deficit, see also: www.Inclusivism.org –and are "win-

win" solutions—the American people win, and capitalism wins!

Jim Green, Democrat candidate for Congress, 2000

PUTTING "COOL" BACK IN THE OBAMA CAMPAIGN:

In the public's mind the words "economy" and "employment" [and in this case "unemployment"] mean one and the same thing—i.e., the Republicans are on to this and are using the word "economy" as code to be derisive towards President Obama—given our horrid 9.1% unemployment rate—

And the handlers saying that we Democrats get an "A" for effort re fixing our unemployment crisis—NO—the public wants RESULTS—and they said this in no uncertain terms during the 2010 election—

The over-arching question re unemployment has turned on "private sector jobs" vs "public sector jobs"—and the administration has gotten bad advice—i.e., it is impossible to say we are on the right path to create private sector jobs when we still have 24 million unemployed/ underemployed in America!

The bottom line is, HR 2847 The HIRE Act [warmed over Reaganomics]—IS NOT WORKING—the result is the PROOF!

David Stockman [a Democrat at heart], former director of OMB [expressing the the Republican mind-set]—even he has on blinders and can see the funding to create jobs as only coming from borrowed money---Really? Where is their Yankee Ingenuity? Where is their imagination?

Capitalism prospers when we have a robust, employed, consuming public—the Republicans say that corporations are not hiring from the $2 trillion in cash they are sitting on—because of Democrat policies—BS—they are not hiring because they need consumers of their products—and we have almost 1 in 10 Americans idle!

Humphrey-Hawkins [15 USC § 3101 - hereafter H-H] is dead-on correct—When our unemployment rises above "3%" our government has an absolute obligation to step up to the plate and create a "reservoir of public employees". We have far more jobs that need to be done, in every jurisdiction in America, than we have persons to fill these jobs--

And, by the government not creating public sector jobs we are asking capitalism to fix our economy, and itself, with both hands tied behind its back—

And rather than throwing our hands up in despair re funding the public sector jobs mandated under H-H— there are numerous methods that will not add a dime to our deficit, or require our borrowing the money—

Rep. Conyers has a Bill in Committee [HR 870] asking Wall Street to fund, and our employed chipping in to help their neighbor [www.Inclusivism.org], to name only two—and we can end our unemployment crisis in 6 months, not 6 years—and stimulate our economy in the process--now that is "COOL"--

Jim Green, Democrat candidate for Congress, 2000

REPUBLICANS: THE TAX CUTS WERE EXTENDED—
WHERE ARE THE JOBS?

President Obama/Fellow Democrats:

The reason we still have 9.2% unemployment is because
those delegated to fix the problem—good intentions
accepted—didn't know how to fix the problem---

The truth is--the world has changed, our solutions
haven't, and the result has been disastrous—

We fail to fix our unemployment crisis because:

1] We fail to see that unemployment is a "social"
problem—capitalism is in the "for profit" business, not in
the "solving social problems" business—and when every
waking moment in capitalism is spent pondering ways to
eliminate as many of us humans, as possible, from the
workplace to increase "profits"—it defies rational human

thought why we would count on [let alone exclusively] "private sector jobs" to solve this "social" problem? The primary role of government is to solve "social" problems-

-

2] We still have on foot on the plantation—the mind-set which frames our policies looks upon humans as entities to be "used and discarded at will"—

3] We failed to account for the "innovation syndrome". We celebrate innovation—but rapidly develop a "deer in the headlights" look re what to do with the 9 persons displaced by the innovation—and the same syndrome applies to automation, globalization, etc. –the Republican solution is to pretend the problem doesn't exist, or admonishes the employee to brush up their resume—

4] We failed to account for how we got where were at— somewhere around the mid-1970's the colliding mega-forces: innovation, technology, automation, globalization, etc., reached a critical mass resulting in ubiquitous unemployment in all of the OECD countries, the US included—and we have been befuddled ever since with what to do with the displaced employee—And the Republican drivel that cutting taxes will create jobs need to be reminded –THE TAX CUTS WERE EXTENDED— WHERE ARE THE JOBS?

5] We fail to recognize that Humphrey-Hawkins [signed by President Carter in 1978] IS the answer—[see also HR 870, currently in Committee]—Specifically, the government has a solemn responsibility to create a "reservoir of public employees—[the "generic job" if you will]" anytime our unemployment rises above "3%"—and we are 3 times over this % at present—

A proposed Senate Bill is The Neighbor-To-Neighbor Job Creation Act: A federally mandated, mutual insurance, owned by our employed—to provide a fund to hire/train our unemployed. Re: www.Inclusivism.org

Jim Green, Democrat candidate for Congress, 2000

F. Michael Kelleher, Special Assistant to the President.

President Obama/Fellow Democrats.

WHY IS HR 870 BEING IGNORED?

It is understandable why we used the TARP and Stimulus tens of billions to swab up the mess caused by Wall Street—to prevent the American economy from going off a cliff—

But we dropped the ball when we did not fix our unemployment crisis--integral to a comprehensive solution—and we are now paying the price—

It is impossible for us to have 9.2% unemployment, and conclude that "conventional wisdom" got right re how to fix our unemployment crisis—

Indeed, we should have put fixing unemployment ahead of fixing Wall Street, in our priorities—because the market thrives when we have a robust, employed, consuming public—and the noted $2 trillion our corporations are sitting on is because they do not have consumers buying their products—

Capitalism is not in the "solving social problems" business [if they want to stay in business]—that is why we don't see them rushing out to hire millions of people [which puzzles our idealists]—when they don't have consumers for their products—

A metaphor re our economic meltdown is a three-legged stool—the Wall Street meltdown, the housing meltdown [with the first two integral to each other], and the employment meltdown—

With the bottom line—had we fixed unemployment, this in kind would have fixed the other two—or conversely: Until we get serious about a WORKABLE SOLUTION for our unemployment crisis—we can forget finding a substantive solution to the Great Recession—

We have a lot of baggage standing in the way of our finding a WORKABLE SOLUTION, including some certifiable members of Congress, nevertheless--

U.S. Representative Conyers has introduced legislation to fix our unemployment crisis, and the only viable solution on our radar: HR 870 [currently in Committee], a latter-day Humphrey Hawkins Full Employment Act [15 USC § 3101, hereafter H-H].

Specifically, H-H authorizes the government/president to create a "reservoir of public employees" anytime our unemployment goes above "3%"—and we can fund without adding a dime to our deficit under HR 870, see also: www.Inclusivism.org

HR 870 is a Pro-Market, "win-win solution"—capitalism wins, and the American people win—So the minute following President Obama signing an Executive Order ending our debt ceiling crisis [if it comes to that] our

next question should be: WHY IS HR 870 BEING
IGNORED?

Jim Green, Democrat candidate for Congress, 2000

CHAPTER TWO: Fail-Safe Electronic Voting

So long as the potential for manipulation of electronic voting continues to exist—our elections in America will be in peril! In spite of all the polls showing a strong Obama victory--it was not until 10PM Central on 11-4-08.....that we could breath a sigh of relief....we had been cheated out of the past two elections....with many believing that Bush was never legally elected president of the United States....and we were braced for the worst.......this can, and MUST be fixed before 2010, so that this never happens again, and in the interest of all who support fair and open elections--regardless of party. Accordingly, it is urged that we adopt the following proposed "FAIL-SAFE ELECTRONIC VOTING ACT":

THE FAIL-SAFE ELECTRONIC VOTING ACT

1) EVERY electronic voting machine (hereafter EVM), must be inexpensive, identical throughout the U.S. in a 1/150 ratio, and *must count and produce a hard-copy of the recorded votes.* In addition, an extra copy of their recorded votes would be produced (not necessarily a hard-copy), marked "Voter's Copy", and containing "NOTICE: Do Not Destroy Until Every Election On Your Ballot Is Certified". [If Wal-Mart refused to give us a receipt for our purchases—would they not be suspect— and this regards our democracy].

2) *After confirming that their votes are recorded correctly,* the voter would then insert the hard-copy ballot into a software-free (count only) optical scanner (hereafter OS), for a second count. The hard-copy ballot would be retained by election officials in the event a candidate asks for a recount (*not possible under the current system, and which undermines the legality of each such election*). The EVM and the OS must be manufactured by different companies (which is universally true today).

3) Election officials assigned to oversee the EVM, would be prevented by law from overseeing the OS, and vice-versa, and stiff criminal penalties would be imposed for violations.

4) Further, every EVM would be programmed with raw data re the total registration rolls, by party, and norms for their voting history, etc.,----as an "alert" to a possible irregularity, such as an "Under-vote"—or "vote-flipping" etc., and *standards* established to suspend certification where there is an "improbable result", at least temporarily, of a particular election until the discrepancy is cleared up. (This is what computers do best, and it would be very easy to create such a program).

5) At the end of the election day, tallies would be taken from the EVM and the OS, for each candidate. *If the tallies didn't balance for any given election, or if there is an "alert", that election cannot be certified until the*

"error" is corrected. If the candidates agree (the victory is certain), minor discrepancies in the count could be disregarded. While probably rare, the Voter, or a random sample of Voters, would be required by law to return their Copy of the recorded votes to the election office to clear up any "error", or where an "alert" signals the need for same.

6) Further, every state provides for a recount when the total vote falls below a certain percent of difference between the candidates, impossible to conduct with the current EVM—and thus Congress must mandate the following regarding presidential candidates: A RUN-OFF election is mandated and triggered in those states where the percent of total vote is less than .5% of difference between any given candidates; said election to be held on the second Saturday following the election, on PAPER BALLOTS ONLY, and contain ONLY the names of the relevant candidates, for instance: "Barack Obama, Democrat" and "John McCain, Republican"—with oversight in counting by a representative(s) of each

party—said procedure providing more than adequate time to meet the Electoral College mandate. NOTE: Had this been the law in 2000, Al Gore would be our president, and the American economy would not be in meltdown!

7) Finally, absent the above safeguards, and until these safeguards are in place--Congress must mandate that PAPER BALLOTS, ONLY, can be used in our presidential elections. This is not a "partisan" issue, it is a "pro-democracy" issue. Most importantly, this will return the responsibility for our elections, and our vote counting, back into the hands of the individual voter, where it belongs, and out of the hands of "corporate control"---*it is after all "our democracy", itself, that is at risk if we don't take these steps---and in that regard, is there any time or cost differential that is too great?*

Reply To: Jim Green -- Democrat candidate for Congress, Dist 21, TX, 2000

jgreen5@satx.rr.com   www.Inclusivism.org

AMENDED/UPDATED:------->The best intentions in the world for the changes the vast majority of Americans agree we need to make--are meaningless, in the absence of fair and honest elections—

PROPOSED PLANK IN THE 2008 DEMOCRATIC NATIONAL PLATFORM

SUBJECT: Election Reform: The "Help America Vote Act" (HAVA), passed by Congress in 2002, has become the Help Republicans Win Act....due to a lack of over-sight of the "private for Profit" corporations that built our Electronic Voting Machines, and then claimed corporate ownership of the software for counting our votes. The Democrat Party supports fair and open elections, and to that end will insist that Congress pass "The Fail-Safe Voting Act", herein above, to protect the integrity of the voting rights of each individual citizen:

President Obama/Fellow Democrats:

A manufacturing job we should start tomorrow is creating a fail-safe electronic machine—or rather system—and have in place by the November election.

Given the known problems with computer security—our democracy is at risk at present, and include "vote-flipping", "under-votes", as well as other deceptions.

Further, there are millions of unspent dollars from HAVA, passed in 2002, and additional funding may not be necessary.

To be viable, a Fail-Safe Electronic Voting System would include:

1] a relatively inexpensive electronic voting machine [hereafter EVM]that would produce a hard copy of the votes we cast, as well as a copy to be retained by the voter and marked "Voter's Copy"—with the votes cast stored on a hard-drive.

2] *After confirming that their votes are recorded correctly,* the voter would then insert the hard-copy ballot into a software-free (count only) optical scanner (hereafter OS), for a second count.

3] At the end of the election day, tallies would be taken from the EVM and the OS, for each candidate. *If the tallies didn't balance for any given election--that election would not be certified unless the "discrepancy" is corrected.*

In many ways, it is inexplicable why it is not mandatory that every voter receive a "Voter's Copy" today, as their receipt—if Wal-Mart handed us a piece of paper with "trust us"—as a receipt for our purchases—we would be outraged, and, here, it is our democracy at risk!

Further, the hard–copy ballot would be retained by election officials in the event a candidate asks for a recount (*not possible under the current system, and which undermines the legality of each such election*).

Election officials assigned to oversee the EVM, would be prevented by law from overseeing the OS, and vice-versa, and stiff criminal penalties would be imposed for violations.

Further, every EVM would be programmed with voting norms as an "alert" to a possible "under-vote" or "vote-flipping" etc., and *standards* established to suspend certification where there is an "improbable result"— [This is what computers do best, and it would be very easy to create such a program].

Finally, in submitting bids we need to look with a jaundiced eye at the bidder. Also, with no government oversight per the FEC—and the Republican "Voter ID" hysteria, with poll-tax fingerprints all over it---and both as a distraction from EVM fraud.....

....what we have now is a nightmare, and our democracy at risk!

Jim Green, Democrat candidate for Congress, 2000

CHAPTER THREE: Miscellaneous -- Self- Explanatory
sent mostly via Facebook

RE: the role of government--Republican policy for the past 30 years, and to this day, is to siphon America's wealth away from the consuming middle—and give it to the already wealthy]via obscene tax cuts—and driving up our deficit]—which has a shelf-life of about 7 years before the economy collapses [1987 & 2008]—In short, anyone voting for Republicans to run our government— is Brain-Dead www.Inclusivism.org

---

Zakaria had opined on his CNN program GPS, that Paul Ryan was "brave" in his corrupt proposed budget cuts which caused this critical response. And question why our media is not honest about Ryan and his ilk---these are "Not Decent People"! Neither is Limbaugh, or most of the Republicans in Congress—their single objective is to pander to the GREED of their wealthiest contributors—

NOT what is in the best interest of the great majority of American, or America!

Fareed Zakaria: You are confusing "brave" with "hypocrisy" in your observation of Ryan's despicable deficit reduction plan. It is very important for us out here in the hinterland to get accurate information [at least some of us]—i.e., "no spin" information from persons we can trust to be accurate—And, unfortunately that took you down a couple of notches because it is Reaganomics—the worst crime ever perpetrated on the American people--on steroids! Among other things, Reaganomics has a shelf-life of about 7 years before the economy starts collapsing in on itself [1987 & 2008]— we can't siphon America's wealth away from the consuming middle without sending our economy into a tailspin, and compounded by increasing the deficit to make up the shortfall in revenue! In short, Ryan's plan would create an America unfit for human habitation— and under no circumstances could it be described as "brave"!

Every one of our economic theories relates to only one species—US, us human beings—and yet not a single theory recognizes the right of us humans to work and be a productive citizen—the most fundamental of our human needs—

Rather, with few exceptions our economic theories are about the "almighty dollar"—and what the almighty dollar can do to make our rich, richer—

In short, us humans are an extraneous footnote—to be used and discarded at will—but always with the end in mind of making the rich, richer—

From Australia, we do have the Buffer Stock Employment Model—which urges an expanding and contracting public workforce—which expands during downturns in the market, and contracts as the market recovers—

THE PSYCHOLOGICAL IMPACT OF UNEMPLOYMENT

The 9.2 unemployment rate is greater than the loss of income for those unemployed. The Zeitgeist is a malaise on the part of the public, and loss of confidence in our economy—in spite of our modest recovery.

RE: the Republican Primaries/Agenda: Turning America back over to the Republicans could be compared to handing the keys to your new Cadillac to a fallen down drunk--who wrecked it last week--in the hopes they will not wreck it again—Surely, the American people are not that stupid? www.Inclusivism.org

---

RE: Ed Henry [who obviously doesn't have enough to do in Hawaii]--For those who ponder if America is on the skids...finis...on our last leg as a great nation—now have their confirmation when a major network wants to pander to our certified idiots—our "birthers" [giving them even 5 seconds of our time, is 5 seconds too long!]—let's do it this way—even if Obama was born on Mars, his mother was a U.S. citizen—which automatically makes him a U.S. citizen—END OF STORY!

The blather that for everyone to have a job we have to create "make work" jobs—is a myth, propaganda BS, our imagination being drowned by a "sacred cow"—the fact is, we have far more work that needs to be done in America, than we have persons to fill these jobs—We do not have a shortage of jobs, we have a shortage of imagination! The Harvard Boys Club on Amazon

---

It is easy to be glib about creating jobs—Romney does it at every speech—so why doesn't anyone in our media ask him, or his campaign, to explain in unequivocal terms how he plans to do that? Does it include cutting taxes for the 1% [how is it distinguished from Bush II]? It is a legitimate "public's right to know" question—required of a "free press"!

The CBO is projecting that following our current trajectory [our current job creation mind-set] that our unemployment will be reduced to 7% by 2015, and 5.5% by 2017—five years from now--This is sad in two ways—first, that anyone would be OK with this—and secondly, because Romney should change his name from Mitt to Hyperbole Romney, because he is trying to snow the American people with a "pipe dream" by sneaking "W's" job creation scheme in through the back door—which was a miserable failure! And what about the consumers our markets will lose out on if we stay on our current course?

The rank and file would do well to heed the warning by President Truman in 1948—that it is us, the American people, who will be the "loser" if we fail to inform ourselves and return America to "VooDoo Economics"1

Many mark America as going off the rails when Bush II was appointed to the presidency—but where America actually went off the rails is when they failed to elect Vice-President Hubert Humphrey to the presidency, in 1968. Humphrey was spot-on correct in his ACCURATE perception of how the world has changed— and what was ESSENTIAL to address these changes. We can go on endlessly in an esoteric discussion, or even emotion/politically driven discussion [and central to this election], about what is—or isn't a "free-enterprise" system—but if we don't get the basics correct—if we don't accurately perceive the problem and how to fix it—we get it wrong, and it would be impossible to have an 8.1% if we got it right....

In a nutshell, with the Republican debates as Exhibit I, re the national Republican agenda this year—If their lips are moving—they are either lying, or they are a hypocrite—and they are counting on the rank and file who vote Republican to have amnesia!

Senator Udall--RE: Newsletter "Winning the Global Economic Race"—3-2-11—until we fix unemployment, all else we do is irrelevant!

Show me a "birther"—I'll show you a "racist"—So why don't we tell the truth—that Trump is trying to incite the ignorant underbelly in America—what is worst about

America—rather than what is best about America? See: The Harvard Boys Club on Amazon www.Inclusivism.org

---

President Obama had a weapon not available to FDR in the war against an economy that had melted away in sheer terror: The Social Security and Military Retirement moneys percolating up through our economy, which not only contributed to Bill Gates becoming the wealthiest man in the world—were it not for these money [Social Security did not start trickling into our economy until 1940]—but were it not for these moneys we would not be talking about having narrowly averted another Great Depression in 2008—We would be buried in one....

ABOUT THE AUTHOR: I was employed in our Criminal Justice System for a cumulative 20 years as a probation officer, with 5 of those years as a chief probation officer. I authored the concept of "Shock Incarceration" which became law in Kansas in 1970, and then was adopted in numerous jurisdictions in the U.S. and also spread to Europe—it is currently identified in the U.S. as "Boot Camp" [as the means to "shock" the young offender—and a total distortion of my original intent—like many ideas, once released, they take on a life of their own]. I was the Democrat candidate for Congress, District 21, TX, 2000. I would most define myself as a Social Ecologist-- [albeit my degree is in Psychology]. My web page is www.Inclusivism.org –which has been on the internet since 1996.